SUMMARY

OF

D0775392

I'll Be Gone in the Dark

Michelle McNamara

By WhizBooks

Table of Contents

Round One: Test Your Memory

"Ready to start the challenge?"

1 POINT EACH

Question #1

Who wrote the introduction to the book?

a. Michael Connelly

b. Gillian Flynn

c. Hillary Clinton

d. Stephen King

ANSWER b

Gillian Flynn

A uthor of the bestselling Girl on the Train ? Gillian Flynn is an admirer of Michele McNamara's work. She notes their similarities-- both of them come from big Irish families, studied in Catholic schools, and fascinated with the dark. Flynn reveals that she feels outmatched by McNamara. While Flynn created her own characters, McNamara wrote about well-researched facts, real-life investigators, and followed the story where it took her. She admired McNamara's doggedness and called her work a beautiful piece of reporting, bringing to life the places, time, and people involved. Unfortunately, Flynn didn't' get to meet McNamara before the latter passed away. Flynn says she wants to know her through the work she has left behind.

Question #2

From where does Mcnamara carry out her hunt for the serial killer using her laptop?

    a. Her office

    b. The local library

    c. Her daughter's playroom

    d. The neighborhood church

ANSWER c

Her daughter's playroom

She would go through the routine of preparing for bedtime, brushing her teeth and wearing her pajamas but instead of going to her bed, she would go to her daughter's playroom and start her sleuthing for the night using her laptop. Her neighborhood near downtown Los Angeles is quiet by that time. She uses Google to check out yearbooks, maps, mugshots, profiles, birth and marriage certificates. She goes through decades old police reports and autopsy files. She is surrounded by her daughter's stuffed toys.

She calls her private searching place a rat's maze. Her notes are all over the place, written with crayon on coloring paper.

Question #3

Who finished this book after McNamara passed away leaving it half-done?

    a.   Billy Jensen and Paul Haynes

    b.   Gillian Flynn

    c.   Stephen King

    d.   Megan Abbot and Michael Connelly

ANSWER a

Billy Jensen and Paul Haynes

Billy Jensen is an investigative journalist hired by McNamara's husband Patton Oswalt. Paul Haynes is McNamara's researcher who had been working with her on the book. She left 3,500 files in her laptop that still had to be put together into narrative. Haynes and Jensen maintained the chapters which McNamara was able to finish and allowed the rest of unfinished drafts to show as a rough project. Some parts appeared as raw transcripts of interviews. Disclaimers were written by Haynes and

13

Jensen in parts where they pieced together the notes. There was no attempt to rewrite or condense her writing into a consistent narrative form.

After the death of McNamara, how long did the writers work on the book before it got published?

a. Two years

b. Three years

c. One year

d. Six months

ANSWER c

One year

Haynes and Jensen worked on the half-finished book for one year before it got published.

They found maps and photos of sites where murders were committed,

Pictures of shoe prints which police found, a spreadsheet containing the identities and addresses of possible links to suspects. They put together these various information that McNamara compiled in order for readers to have a clear view of what she was doing.

McNamara was convinced that DNA and genealogy are the keys to identifying the serial killer who has evaded the police for decades. Hayes and Jensen explored this avenue. Haynes, who was shocked by McNamara's sudden demise, thinks she was very ambitious in writing the book. It had a very wide scope and he wondered which holes they can cover.

Why did Roger Harrington consult a clairvoyant?

a. He wanted to know beforehand what will happen to
the murderer.

b. He wanted to know his future.

c. He desperately wanted to know who killed his son;
the police do not have answers.

d. He wanted to know if he would succeed.

ANSWER c

He desperately wanted to know who killed his son; the

police do not have answers.

Roger Harrington is the father of Keith and father-in-law of Patty, who were both murdered in their home at Dana Point in

Orange County, in 1980.

He found them dead in their bedroom. Investigators

considered the theory that the killer could be the same

one who killed Manuela Witthuhn in Irvine six months

before. But no suspect was caught. After 10 years and

finding no forthcoming leads from the police, he hired a

private investigator to look further into the case. He offered a big reward hoping to entice anybody who could offer a clue. But nothing came up. Finally, despite him being a tough and practical businessman, he decided to consult a clairvoyant. Still, this led to no result. There was nothing that could illuminate him on why his son and daughter-in-law were killed violently.

Question #6

Who is Drew Witthuhn?

a. A suspect for a crime committed in Irvine in 1981.

b. The husband of a murder victim

c. the father of the murdered Manuela

d. the brother-in-law of the murdered Manuela

ANSWER d

the brother-in-law of the murdered Manuela

D rew Witthuhn is the brother of David who was married to Manuela, found dead in their bedroom in Northwood, Irvine. It was February 1981. Drew was a police-in-training then and it was him who cleaned up the bedroom of blood splattered on the bed and wall after the police were done collecting evidence. His older brother was confined at the hospital when the crime happened. He described Manuela as brusque. Drew was jealous of David and Manuela's success. They had well-paying jobs and bought their house which was located in a new subdivision. Drew felt inconsequential compared to them. After cleaning scene of the crime, Drew unwillingly burst into tears.

What did the Golden State Killer do before carrying out his crimes?

a.   He called his victims

a. He preplanned his attack

b. He delivered pizza to the house

c. He befriended his victims

ANSWER b

He preplanned his attack

The Golden State Killer is described by McNamara as precise and self-preserving. He broke into homes long before committing his crimes, studying the layout, pictures, location of light switches, emptying guns of their bullets. He made sure he could easily enter and leave the house by leaving gates open and sliding doors unlocked. Before the night of Manuela Witthuhn's murder, David Witthuhn noticed shoe marks around his house three or four months before the crime. The police found the same description of shoe marks in the crime scene. McNamara wrote that Manuela's murder shows signs of preplanning. There were ligatures that had been cut and prepared beforehand.

Question #8

What did the golden state killer say when he called one of his victims on the phone 24 years after he raped her?

a. "Remember when we played?"

b. "Do you remember me?"

c. "Are your parents' home?"

d. "How have you been?"

ANSWER a

"Remember when we played?"

The Golden State killer continued to terrorize his victims despite becoming inactive for almost a decade. In 2001, a woman who was victimized 24 years ago received a call from a man who sounded familiar. He asked: "Remember when we played?" The woman recognized his voice right away. McNamara thinks he uses similar language with his other victims. A six year old girl woke up one night and saw a man wearing a ski mask, black mittens, and had no pants on. He wore a belt with a sword dangling underneath. He told the little girl: "I'm playing tricks with your mom and

dad. Come watch me."

Who wrote the Afterword?

a. Michelle McNamara

b. Patton Oswalt

c. Billy Jensen

d. Paul Haynes

ANSWER b

Patton Oswalt

P atton Oswalt writes in the Afterword that he and his wife shared the same passion for serial killers. McNamara knew the minute details about famous movies and real life characters related to serial killers. But unlike Oswalt who collected these dark details, McNamara treated them like background noise, not the important part. She focused on the detectives and investigators who dealt with clues and trapped the killers with their expert sleuthing. Oswalt witnessed how his wife got angry reading victims' testimonies. Or how she despaired after interviewing families of victims. She wept after realizing that a lead she had been following resulted to a dead end.

Question #10

Why does McNamara believe that the killer will soon be caught?

a. Somebody has tipped his identity and whereabouts.

b. He will be overwhelmed with guilt and will confess his crimes.

c. He will commit one more crime and this time he will be caught.

d. The technologies of connectivity, speed and DNA profiling will lead to his capture.

33

ANSWER d

The technologies of connectivity, speed and DNA profiling will lead to his capture.

In her *Epilogue: Letter to an Old Man*, Mcnamara tells the killer that the tables have been turned, his prowess and skills are of no value anymore. Virtual windows have opened that will lead to his capture. She mentions the development of DNA profiling in 1984, the World Wide Web proposed in 1989. Google came into being in 1998. This all led to the scanning and digitizing of police reports. People who didn't know him have devised algorithms that will track him down. One day, a police car will come to get him, like it did with other criminals who were caught 20 or 30 years after their last crimes.

Who is Fred Ray?

a. He is McNamara's brother

b. He is a retired detective

c. He is one of the victims

d. He is her brother-in-law

ANSWER b

He is a retired detective

F red Ray is retired detective that McNamara interviewed about a double murder that happened 35 years ago. She describes him as a tall, laconic man with long fingers and abundant brown hair. She met him in a tiny cafe filled with Swedish-made stuff, in Kingsburg, California. Ray worked at the office of the Santa Barbara County Sheriff. He apprehended young people who prowled homes, entering houses without the owners' knowledge and watched them unseen. He doesn't think one of them was the

Golden State killer though he tried to track him one night in the neighborhood, through his shoe prints. He believed the police could have caught him one night as he tried to escape, but he knew the deputies will let him slip away.

Question #12

What document did McNamara modify three days before she died?

a. A document titled "FinishedDrafts"

b. A list of suspects

c. A list of victims

d. A document titled "StillToDo"

ANSWER d

A document titled "StillToDo"

McNamara had a document titled "StillToDo" which she updated three days before she died. The list included:

1. Ask Debbi D about flashlight, and if Greg visited Toltec.

2. Ask detective Ray why Offerman/Manning crime is worse than the Domingo/Sanchez crime. A detective had to take psychiatric leave after said crime.

3. Ask Erika what does she think happened at Cruz crime.

4. Ask Ken Clark about public link to Maggiore homicide; about FBI familial hits; about clown walking down the road.

She had many questions for the detectives and investigators. She was determined to follow each lead and fit every piece. Detectives were able to trust her, a feat that is normally hard to accomplish.

According to Ken Clark, what was McNamara able to accomplish with her sleuthing?

a. She led police to the killer's identity

b. She called attention to a serial killer who was prolific yet least known.

c. She caused the killer to confess

d. She roused fears of a serial killer yet to be caught

ANSWER b

She called attention to a serial killer who was prolific yet least known.

Ken Clark said McNamara had an unquestionable impact on the case of the Golden State Killer. She called attention to the case of a serial killer who was among those who had committed such a high number of crimes in American crime history, and yet is the least known. Her research and stories seemed unbelievable yet Clark saw that she was on track. Clark cited her impeccable research skills, her propensity for detail and impassioned desire to have the criminal identified. These qualities enabled her to interview the victims and their families with their privacy intact and at the same time culling for more information about the suspect.

Was the Golden State Killer eventually caught?

a. Yes

b. No

c. Yes but he is not the real killer

d. No he had been dead for years

ANSWER a

Yes

Hours before Mcnamara's husband Patton Oswalt announced that he believed the killer will be caught soon, the police arrested the man they think is the Golden State Killer. His name is Joseph James DeAngelo, 72. Oswalt was promoting McNamara's book when he uttered his prediction. DeAngelo was arrested for committing two of the murders associated to the Golden State Killer. Police soon confirmed that he is the killer that McNamara had been tracking for the past few years of her life before she passed away. Police cited DNA as evidence. Oswalt said that the arrest felt a deeply personal event for him. He was elated that the killer was finally identified, but he also felt sad that his late wife was not there to witness the happy event.

Who said "There is a scream permanently lodged in my throat now" ?

a. Manuela Witthuhn

b. Ken Clark

c. Michelle McNamara

d. Patton Oswalt

ANSWER c

Michelle McNamara

Michelle McNamara had been warned by a fellow investigator she calls the Social Worker to watch out and take care of herself because the work can consume her. But she was already consumed. She wrote that "there's a scream permanently lodged in my throat now." She had become paranoid. One time she thought somebody snuck into her room while she was sleeping. She swung the nightstand lamp at the man's head, only to find out in the morning that it was her husband who tiptoed into bed so as not to awaken her. She admitted her own obsession with the case, calling it mania. It led her to dangerous situations. Her sleep and health were very much affected.

Round Two: How Well Do You Know the Author?

"Let's get personal."

2 POINTS EACH

Question #1

How did Michelle McNamara came up with the idea of writing a book about the Golden State Killer?

a. She wrote for the *New York Times* about crime.

b. She created the website TrueCrimeDiary and published crime articles in Los Angeles magazine.

c. She wrote a suspense thriller before turning to true crime.

d. She was editor of suspense thriller books.

ANSWER b

She created the website TrueCrimeDiary and published crime articles in Los Angeles magazine.

McNamara had always been interested in crime solving since childhood when her neighbor's murder remained unresolved. After taking an MFA in creative writing and moving to Hollywood to write for tv and film projects, she created the website TrueCrimeDiary. She wrote articles about the serial killer whom she eventually called The Golden State Killer. The articles were published in Los Angeles magazine. She appeared on an interactive panel which featured citizens using social media to help solve murders. Harper Collins then inked a book deal with her as she continued to investigate the case. The book, entitled *I'll Be Gone in the Dark: One Woman's Obsessive Search for the Golden State Killer,* was published almost two years after her death.

How did McNamara die?

a. She had a heart condition that caused blocked arteries.

b. She had a nightmare she did not wake up from.

c. She had breast cancer.

d. She had a brain aneurysm.

ANSWER a

She had a heart condition that caused blocked arteries.

❦

McNamara had a heart condition she never knew about. She had blocked arteries which caused her death on April 21, 2016, when her husband Patton Oswalt found her in bed. She was found to have been taking Adderall, Xanax, and Fentanyl— medication for ADD/ADHD, anxiety, and pain respectively. Her husband said she had insomnia and showed panicky behavior. Once she woke up panicked in the middle of the night to the sound of a neighbor unloading garbage. She had an overloaded mind. The psychological stress of pursuing a criminal which "gave her a scream lodged in her throat" took its toll. Oswalt did not realize that she coped with the stress by taking medication.

What is her website True Crime Diary about?

a. It is about crime sources for suspense thrillers.

b. It is about her online research about unresolved

crimes

c. It is about her favorite mystery thriller stories.

d. It is about police detectives and their work.

It is about her online research about unresolved crimes

M cNamara created the website in order to write and document her ongoing online research on unsolved crimes. She had been looking into social media for information about suspects. She discovered that sociopaths and narcissists who have committed crimes easily revealed themselves through Twitter, Facebook, and Tumblr accounts. Google Maps served useful in locating geographic data. She linked seemingly unconnected cases from different states. TV news programs noticed her website and used her expertise to pursue crime-related news stories. In 2011, she started writing about rapes and murders that happened in the 70s and 80s. This led to the discovery that these were committed by a single man known as the East Area Rapist and Original Night Stalker.

Question #4

McNamara confesses that she would rather go home early rather than stay longer at a Hollywood event which her husband is part of. Why?

a. She has to sleep early for an early morning event next day.

b. She wants to go back to her laptop to search for more information about a murderer.

c. She hates Hollywood

b. She's going back to her three-month old baby

ANSWER b

She wants to go back to her laptop to search for more information about a murderer.

Her husband is actor Patton Oswalt. She joins him during the premiere of *Funny People*. She relates how dazed and exhilarated she is during the event as she rubs elbows with famous celebrities. She explains that she is not being falsely humble by saying it's not her thing to attend Hollywood events. Attending such events is part of her wife duties, she being married to an actor whom she loves, and whose movies she admires. But she is also preoccupied with her ongoing research for a murderer. She makes people believe that they're going home early for their three-month old baby, but the truth is "much weirder," she says. She is going back to her laptop to continue searching for a murderer.

Question #5

Where did McNamara grow up?

a. Northwood, Irvine

b. Oak Park, Chicago

c. Dana Point, Orange County

d. Sacramento, County

ANSWER b

Oak Park, Chicago

She grew up in Oak Park, Chicago. Her family lived in a three-story Victorian house. Her parents belonged to the tribe called West Side Irish. She described her father as a jolly man, and her mother, a teetotaler who comes from a family who loved to drink. Her mother was fascinated with Judy Garland and Hollywood. Her family attended the St. Edmund Catholic Church, which was also her school till third grade. Her father took up Law at Northwestern Law School and worked at Jenner and Block law firm for nearly 40 years. She was the youngest in a family of six where she felt like she arrived in the family just when the party was winding down.

Question #6

With whom did she have her most complicated relationship in her life?

    a. Her father

    b. Her eldest sister

    c. her mother

    d. Her husband

ANSWER c

her mother

McNamara wanted her mother's approval but she also felt suffocated. Her mother was proud of her for being strong-minded but she often felt slighted when her daughter used her sharp mind against her. It was painful for McNamara to think that her mother would have been happy that she had a book about to be published but she also felt would be difficult to write if her mother were still alive. When she gave birth to her daughter Alice, she finally understood her mother's love for her. She cried hysterically and asked her husband to look for the letter

her mom wrote her when they had their biggest fight.

What led McNamara to get interested in sleuthing?

a. She read Nancy Drew mysteries.

b. The murder of her relatives.

c. The unresolved murder of her neighbor Kathleen

Lombardo.

d. She liked to read Sherlock Holmes.

ANSWER c

The unresolved murder of her neighbor Kathleen

Lombardo.

The murder of her neighbor Kathleen Lombardo when she was in her early teens was forever etched in her memory. The crime remained unresolved. Two days after the crime she walked to the place where it happened near their house. She picked up broken pieces of the Walkman that Kathleen wore when she went jogging that night. She felt a strong curiosity as she looked around the place where the crime happened. She wanted to see the face of the man who did it. Since then she was obsessed with murders that had no resolutions. She started hoarding details that she hoped could fit together. She borrowed books about the macabre and true.

Reminder: Claim Your Free Books

Dear reader,

If you haven't already, don't forget to claim your free download of our *All-Time Top 5 Best Sellers* absolutely free as a part of this purchase.

Get Your Bonus Download Here.

Just enter where you want the books to be digitally delivered.

Editors at
WhizBooks

The Moment of Truth

Results May Vary

Based on the difficulty of these questions:

Less than 5 points wrong – Expert – Congratulations! You've passed the challenge with flying colors

Less than 15 points wrong – Knowledgeable – You are very familiar with the topic.

Less than 30 points wrong – Rookie – Barely passed the challenge, you can do better next time.

Play Again?

The First Challenge

The Second Challenge

or

The Epilogue

The Epilogue:

"In Case You Missed It"

I'll Be Gone in the Dark: One Woman's Obsessive Search for the Golden State Killer* is Michelle McNamara's posthumous book that documents her sleuthing work tracking a murderer who hounded California residents in the 70s and 80s. It was an obsession that preoccupied her for a decade and which eventually led to her death, caused by an undiagnosed heart condition exacerbated by the stress and anxiety that her work incurred. Almost two years after her death, her book was published on February 2018. This was followed on April 2018 by the capture of Joseph James DeAngelo on whom the police found DNA evidence for having committed the rapes and murders attributed to the Golden State Killer.

The book chronicles the deaths that happened in middle-class neighborhoods in Irvine, Sacramento, Dana Point and in areas nearing these. McNamara tells the stories of the victims from the point of view of family members and police investigators who worked on the cases. Using online research with Google Maps, Twitter, Facebook, Tumblr, blogs and other social media apps she gathered information that enabled her to make a sketchy profile of the Golden State Killer. The man always entered the house to do some preplanning before carrying out his crime, familiarizing himself with the would-be victims and the house. He is white, athletic and always wore a mask. He had size nine shoes and his blood type is A. He had a small penis and he cried after committing his brutal acts. McNamara died in 2016 leaving the book half-finished. It was finalized by Billy Jensen, an investigative journalist, and Paul Haynes, McNamara's researcher who had been working with her on the book. She left 3,500 files in her laptop that still had to be put together into narrative.

A part of the book is written as a memoir, giving an account of the author's childhood and family. She wrote a moving account of her conflicted relationship with her late mother. She related how the unsolved murder of a neighbor piqued her interest in wanting to solve mysterious crimes. Her honesty shone through as she spoke about her obsession and was aware that her health was endangered. Her stories of the victims' relatives who shared to her their experience and insights about the crimes were flawlessly told, compelling, and full of empathy. She put much effort in getting to know the detectives, the survivors and even the Golden State Killer whose face and character she kept trying to figure out. Haynes and Jensen maintained the chapters which McNamara finished and allowed the rest of unfinished drafts to show as a rough project. Some parts appeared as raw transcripts of interviews. Disclaimers were written by Haynes and Jensen in parts where they pieced together the notes. There was no attempt to rewrite or condense her unfinished writing into a consistent narrative form. The introduction is written by bestselling psychological thriller author Gillian Flynn who confessed feeling outdone by McNamara. The Afterword is given by her husband Patton Oswalt who revealed that their passion for serial killers brought them together. The importance of recent technology is highlighted in the book. In her *Epilogue: Letter to an Old Man*, Mcnamara tells the killer that his prowess and skills are of no value anymore. Virtual windows have opened that will lead to his capture. She mentions the development of DNA profiling in 1984, the World Wide Web proposed in 1989. Google came into being in 1998. This all led to the scanning and digitizing of police reports. People who didn't know him have devised algorithms that will track him down. One day, a police car will come to get him, like it did with other criminals who were caught 20 or 30 years after their last crimes.

The book is a *New York Times* bestseller in the nonfiction print and e-book category, staying on the list for eight weeks as of April 2018. HBO has purchased the rights for the book and has started working on a documentary series based on it with Liz Garbus as director.

McNamara had an MFA in creative writing and wrote for tv and film projects. She created the website TrueCrimeDiary.com. She wrote articles about the serial killer published in Los Angeles magazine. When she died, she was found to have been taking Adderall, Xanax, and Fentanyl— medication for ADD/ADHD, anxiety, and pain respectively. Her husband said she had insomnia and showed panicky behavior. The psychological stress of pursuing a criminal who "gave her a scream forever lodged in her throat" took its toll.

She grew up in Oak Park, Chicago.

Last Chance for Bonus Download

Dear reader,

If you haven't already, this is the last chance to download our *All-Time Top 5 Best Sellers* absolutely free for you absolutely free as a part of this purchase.

Get Your Bonus Download Here.

We hope you have enjoyed this book.

Please take a moment to leave a review when you're done and share your experience.

Editors at

WhizBooks

CPSIA information can be obtained
at www.ICGtesting.com
Printed in the USA
LVHW020327190520
656030LV00019B/1635